PRAYER
(Abendsegen)
from *Hänsel und Gretel*

Arranged by Henry Charles Smith

Engelbert Humperdinck
(1854-1921)

Trombone

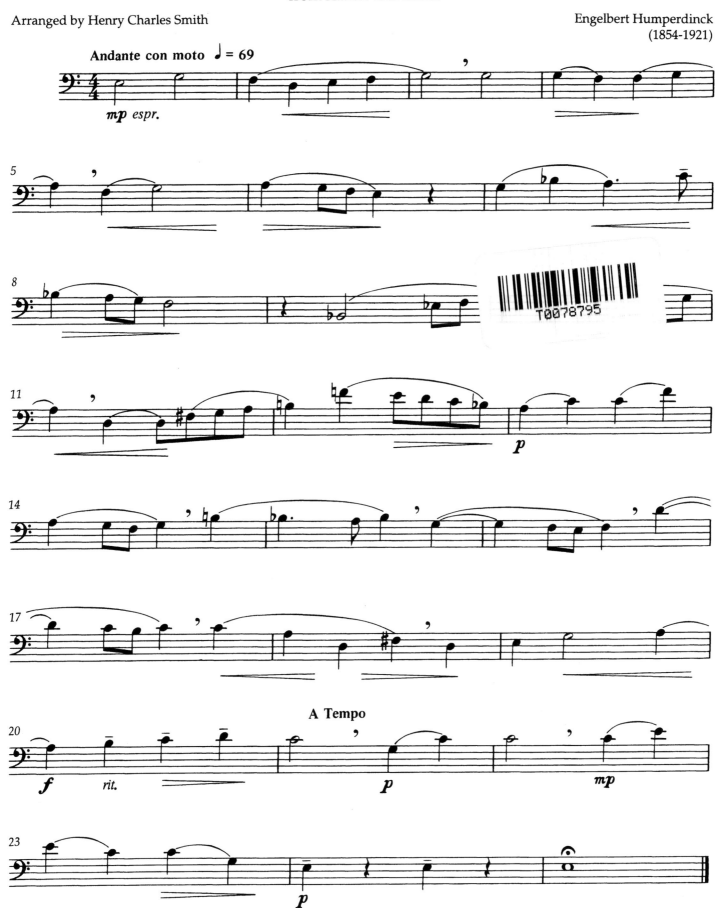

Copyright © 1989 by HAL LEONARD PUBLISHING CORPORATION
International Copyright Secured ALL RIGHTS RESERVED Printed in the U.S.A.

CANTATE DOMINO
from *Musica Divina*

Trombone

Arranged by Henry Charles Smith

Giuseppe Ottavio Pitoni
(1657-1743)

*Play the piece twice through; no ritard. nor fermata the first time.

Copyright © 1989 by HAL LEONARD PUBLISHING CORPORATION
International Copyright Secured ALL RIGHTS RESERVED Printed in the U.S.A.

GAVOTTE
from Suite for Unaccompanied Violoncello No. 6 in D Major, BWV 1012

Trombone

Arranged by Henry Charles Smith

Johann Sebastian Bach
(1685-1750)

Copyright © 1989 by HAL LEONARD PUBLISHING CORPORATION
International Copyright Secured ALL RIGHTS RESERVED Printed in the U.S.A.

14 COLLECTED INTERMEDIATE QUINTETS

THE CANADIAN BRASS

THE LIBERTY BELL

ombone

Arranged by Henry Charles Smith

John Philip Sousa
(1854-1932)

Copyright © 1989 by HAL LEONARD PUBLISHING CORPORATION
International Copyright Secured ALL RIGHTS RESERVED Printed in the U.S.A.

THE DRUNKEN SAILOR

Trombone

Arranged by Terry Vosbein

Traditional

Copyright © 1989 by HAL LEONARD PUBLISHING CORPORATION
International Copyright Secured ALL RIGHTS RESERVED Printed in the U.S.A.

GREENSLEEVES

ombone

Arranged by Terry Vosbein

Traditional

Copyright © 1989 by HAL LEONARD PUBLISHING CORPORATION
International Copyright Secured ALL RIGHTS RESERVED Printed in the U.S.A.

HAVA NAGILA

Trombone

Arranged by Walter Barnes

Traditional

© Copyright 1988 Dr. Brass (BMI), Toronto
All Rights reserved. Printed in U.S.A.
Unauthorized copying, arranging, recording or public performance is an infringement of copyright.
Infringers are liable under the law.

HIGH BARBARY

Trombone

Arranged by Terry Vosbein

Traditional

Copyright © 1989 by HAL LEONARD PUBLISHING CORPORATION
International Copyright Secured ALL RIGHTS RESERVED Printed in the U.S.A.

JUST A CLOSER WALK

Trombone

Arranged by Don Gillis
Adapted by Walter Barnes

Traditional

© Copyright 1988 Dr. Brass (BMI), Toronto
All Rights reserved. Printed in U.S.A.
Unauthorized copying, arranging, recording or public performance is an infringement of copyright.
Infringers are liable under the law.

LONDONDERRY AIR

Arranged by Terry Vosbein

Traditional

Trombone

Copyright © 1989 by HAL LEONARD PUBLISHING CORPORATION
International Copyright Secured ALL RIGHTS RESERVED Printed in the U.S.A.

SHENANDOAH

Trombone

Arranged by Terry Vosbein

Traditional

Copyright © 1989 by HAL LEONARD PUBLISHING CORPORATION
International Copyright Secured ALL RIGHTS RESERVED Printed in the U.S.A.

SIMPLE GIFTS

Trombone

Arranged by Terry Vosbein

Traditional

Copyright © 1989 by HAL LEONARD PUBLISHING CORPORATION
International Copyright Secured ALL RIGHTS RESERVED Printed in the U.S.A.

THIS AND THAT
(Questo e quella)
from *Rigoletto*

Trombone

Arranged by Henry Charles Smith

Giuseppe Verdi
(1813-1901)

Copyright © 1989 by HAL LEONARD PUBLISHING CORPORATION
International Copyright Secured ALL RIGHTS RESERVED Printed in the U.S.A.

PILGRIM'S CHORUS
from *Tannhäuser und der Sängerkrieg auf Wartburg*

Trombone

Arranged by Henry Charles Smith

Richard Wagner
(1813-1883)

Copyright © 1989 by HAL LEONARD PUBLISHING CORPORATION
International Copyright Secured ALL RIGHTS RESERVED Printed in the U.S.A.

CONTENTS

JOHANN SEBASTIAN BACH

SCORE AND PARTS AVAILABLE SEPARATELY:

Conductor's Score	50486959
Trumpet 1 in B-flat	50486954
Trumpet 2 in B-flat	50486955
Horn in F	50486956
Tuba	50486958

ALSO AVAILABLE IN THIS SERIES:
17 Collected Easy Quintets   50486953

U.S. $12.99

HAL•LEONARD®
CORPORATION
7777 W. BLUEMOUND RD. P.O. BOX 13819 MILWAUKEE, WI 53213

www.canbrass.com
www.halleonard.com

ISBN 978-1-4234-8424-0

HL50486957